The Lighthouse Book

The Lighthouse Book

Michael Berenstain

David McKay Company, Inc.

New York

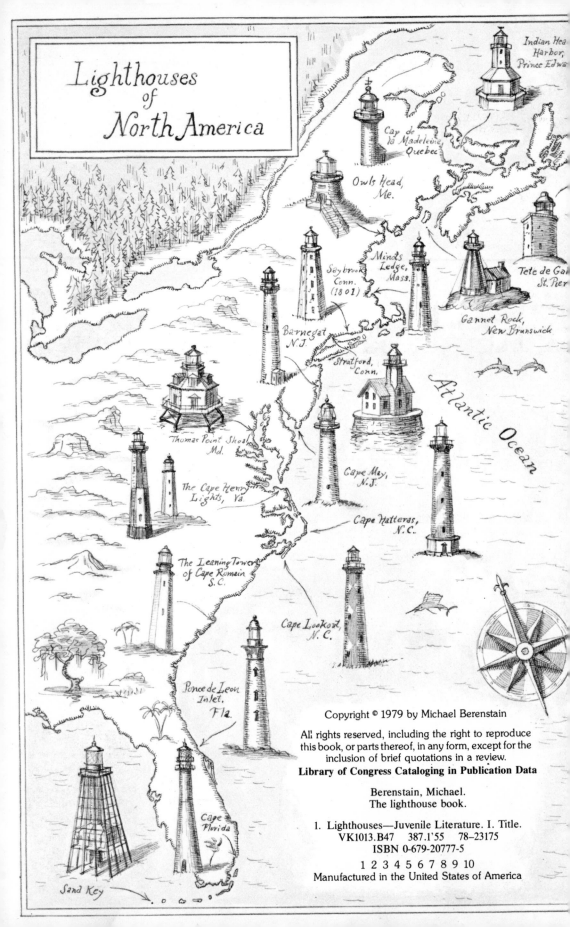

Lighthouses
of
North America

Indian Head Harbor, Prince Edwa[rd]

Cap de la Madeleine Quebec

Owls Head, Me.

Minds Ledge, Mass.

Saybrook Conn. (1801)

Tete de Ga[lantry] St. Pier[re]

Gannet Rock, New Brunswick

Barnegat N.J.

Stratford, Conn.

Thomas Point Shoal Md.

Cape May, N.J.

The Cape Henry Lights, Va.

Cape Hatteras, N.C.

The Leaning Tower of Cape Romain S.C.

Cape Lookout, N.C.

Ponce de Leon Inlet, Fla.

Cape Florida

Sand Key

Atlantic Ocean

Library of Congress Cataloging in Publication Data

Berenstain, Michael.
The lighthouse book.

1. Lighthouses—Juvenile Literature. I. Title.
VK1013.B47   387.1'55   78-23175
ISBN 0-679-20777-5

1 2 3 4 5 6 7 8 9 10
Manufactured in the United States of America

Since ancient times, fishermen have set sail at dawn and returned to port at sunset. The ancestor of the modern lighthouse may well have been a bonfire that guided fishing boats home after dark.

This crude source of light might have served the needs of fishermen, but as ships made longer and longer voyages, better lights were needed.

The first lighthouses probably were simple stone towers at the entrances of harbors. They might have been used, too, as signal or watch towers.

One of the earliest, and by far the largest, of all lighthouses was the Pharos of Alexandria. Built about 2,300 years ago, it rose to a height of over 400 feet. Its lowest level was a fortress. Its highest level housed the beacon: an open fire magnified by a giant mirror.

This vast work of ancient Egypt was so famous that its name has come to mean lighthouse in many languages.

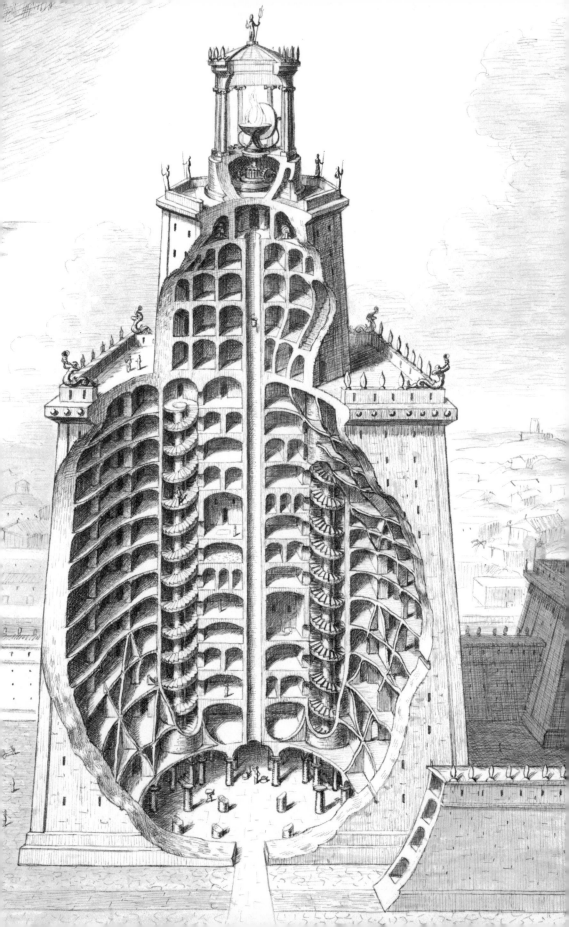

The Pharos was one of the Seven Wonders of the Ancient World. It guided ships in the eastern Mediterranean for over a thousand years until, finally, it was destroyed, partly by Arab invaders, partly by earthquake.

Today, not a stone remains.

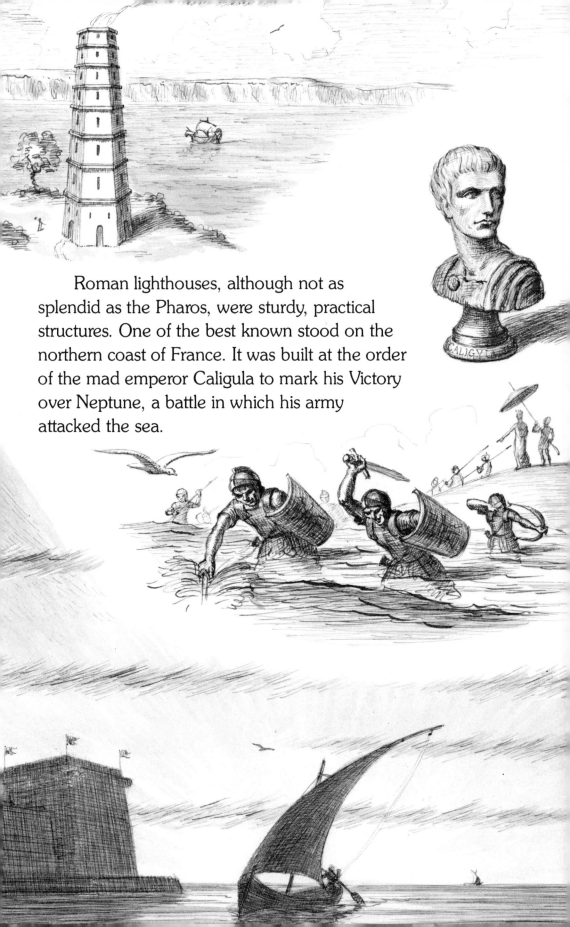

Roman lighthouses, although not as splendid as the Pharos, were sturdy, practical structures. One of the best known stood on the northern coast of France. It was built at the order of the mad emperor Caligula to mark his Victory over Neptune, a battle in which his army attacked the sea.

After the fall of Rome, most old lighthouses were neglected and fell into ruin. No new ones were built.

But in the 1100s, sea trade began to revive, creating a need for new lighthouses. One of the best built at this time was at Genoa.

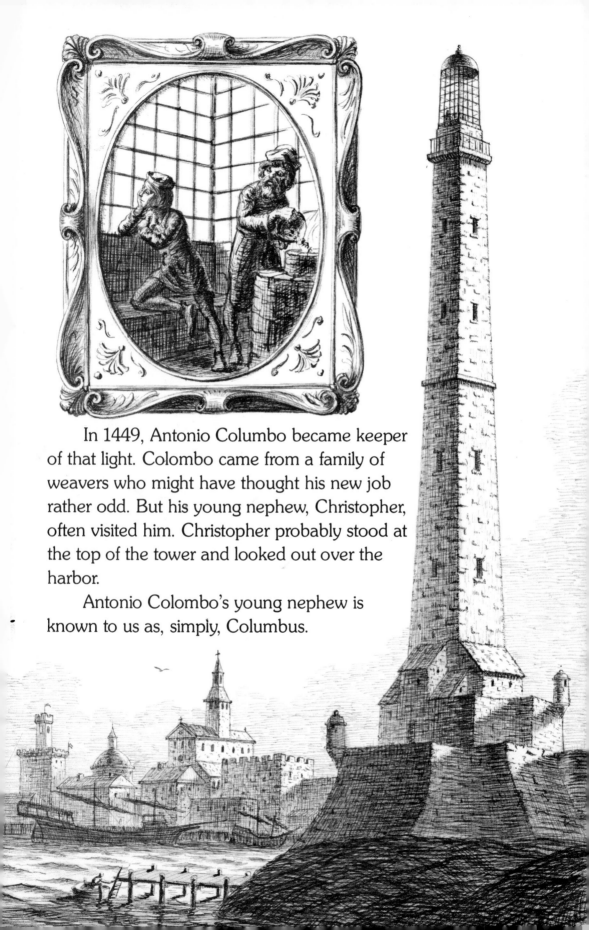

In 1449, Antonio Columbo became keeper of that light. Colombo came from a family of weavers who might have thought his new job rather odd. But his young nephew, Christopher, often visited him. Christopher probably stood at the top of the tower and looked out over the harbor.

Antonio Colombo's young nephew is known to us as, simply, Columbus.

One of the greatest danger to ships at sea are rocks and reefs. These are places where lighthouses are the most difficult to build. It was not until 1584 that a lighthouse was erected on such a spot: the tiny isle of Cordouan off the coast of France.

Without doubt, it was the most elaborate lighthouse since the Pharos. In addition to the light and keepers' quarters, it had an entrance hall, a chapel, and a royal apartment for the King in case he paid a visit (he never did).

This building was a great work, but even more amazing were the series of lighthouses built on the Eddystone rocks off Plymouth, England.

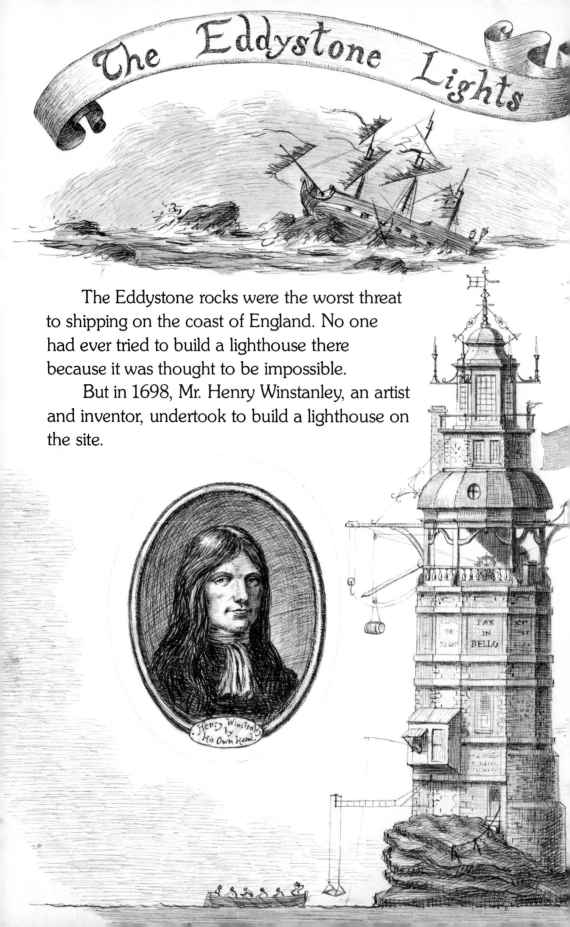

The Eddystone Lights

The Eddystone rocks were the worst threat to shipping on the coast of England. No one had ever tried to build a lighthouse there because it was thought to be impossible.

But in 1698, Mr. Henry Winstanley, an artist and inventor, undertook to build a lighthouse on the site.

Henry Winstanley
by His Own Hand

Some thought him mad—not only because of his project. His home was like a fun house, complete with trap doors, trick chairs, and the like. He called it Winstanley's Wonders and charged admission.

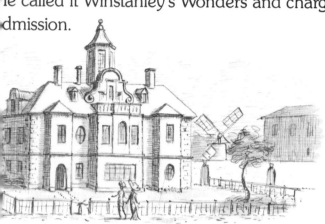

But, mad or not, he did build his lighthouse. To those who said it would blow away, he replied that he wished nothing better than to be inside it during "the greatest storm that ever was."

On November 26, 1703, while making repairs inside the lighthouse, he got his wish. A violent storm struck, and the entire building and Mr. Henry Winstanley were swept away.

A few years later, another light was built. Although it had a more sensible design than the last, it also had one serious flaw: it was made of wood. After fifty years of service, it was destroyed by fire.

Ye Destruction of Ye Eddystone Light

Still another tower was then built, thi time by one of the great engineers of the day, John Smeaton. Constructed with interlocking blocks of granite, it was the first truly modern lighthouse.

A Typical Course of Masonry

Because the rock had eroded after 120 years, Smeaton's tower had to be replaced. A new tower was built nearby, and most of the old lighthouse was torn down. Its upper portion was re-erected in Plymouth, but its base still stands on the Eddystone rocks.

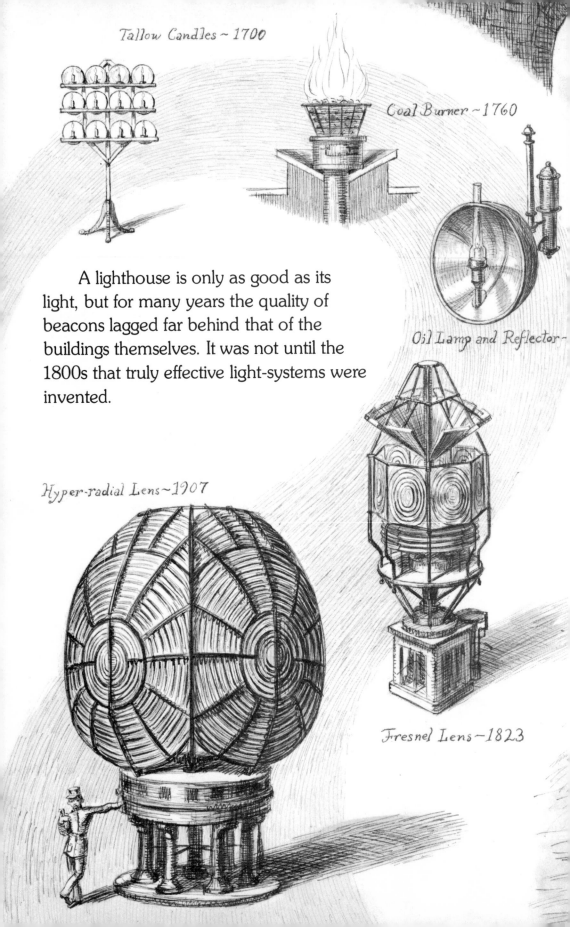

Tallow Candles ~ 1700

Coal Burner ~ 1760

Oil Lamp and Reflector ~

A lighthouse is only as good as its light, but for many years the quality of beacons lagged far behind that of the buildings themselves. It was not until the 1800s that truly effective light-systems were invented.

Hyper-radial Lens ~ 1907

Fresnel Lens — 1823

Not even the brightest lights can pierce dense fog, so sound signals are also needed. The earliest warning signals may have been bells—probably those of seaside temples or churches.

Cannon, too, were tried. But, in fog, it was hard to judge the distance of their short blasts.

Nowadays, compressed air horns are used. The first types were steam powered and had huge mouths.

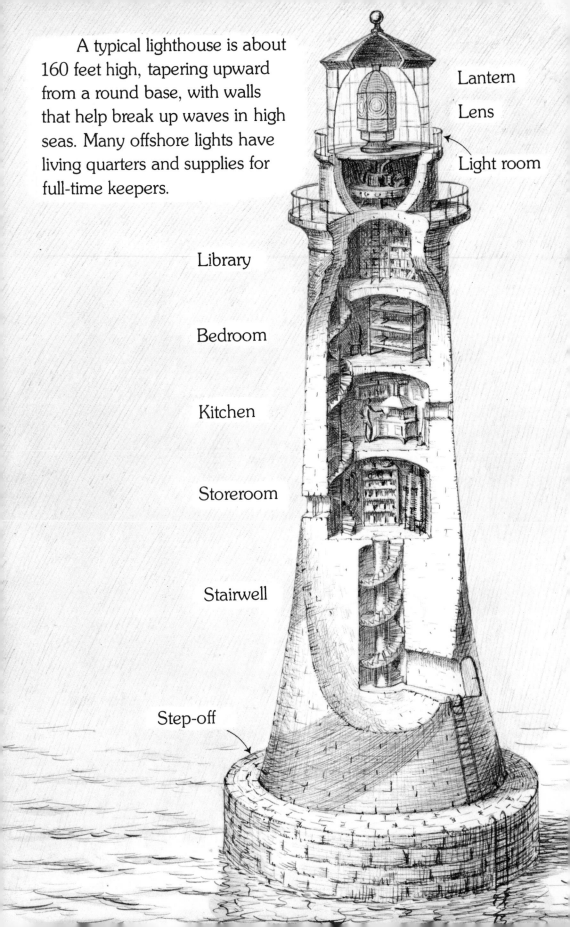

A typical lighthouse is about 160 feet high, tapering upward from a round base, with walls that help break up waves in high seas. Many offshore lights have living quarters and supplies for full-time keepers.

Lantern

Lens

Light room

Library

Bedroom

Kitchen

Storeroom

Stairwell

Step-off

Life in a lighthouse isn't easy. A visitor to one may find just reaching it difficult.

Once there, getting inside is another problem.

The lower part of the tower is solid stone, with a narrow spiral staircase leading to the upper floors.

The first floor is a storeroom, where food, water, fuel, and other supplies are kept.

Above the storeroom is the kitchen. It's customary for the keepers to take turns at cooking.

To save space in the bedroom, bunk beds are the rule. Sometimes there are spare bunks for visitors.

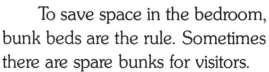

Some lighthouses, especially
the oldest ones, have large
libraries. Those that don't are sent
collections of books, which rotate
among the various lights.

When off duty, the keepers may try
their hands at kite-fishing. It's thought that
this sport was invented at the old
Eddystone light.

At the top of the tower is the light room—the reason for and the purpose of the entire structure. Most of a keeper's time is spent here, caring for the lamp and its housing.

The life of a lighthouse keeper is often dull and lonely. But perhaps the beauty and mystery of the surrounding sea partly makes up for this drawback.

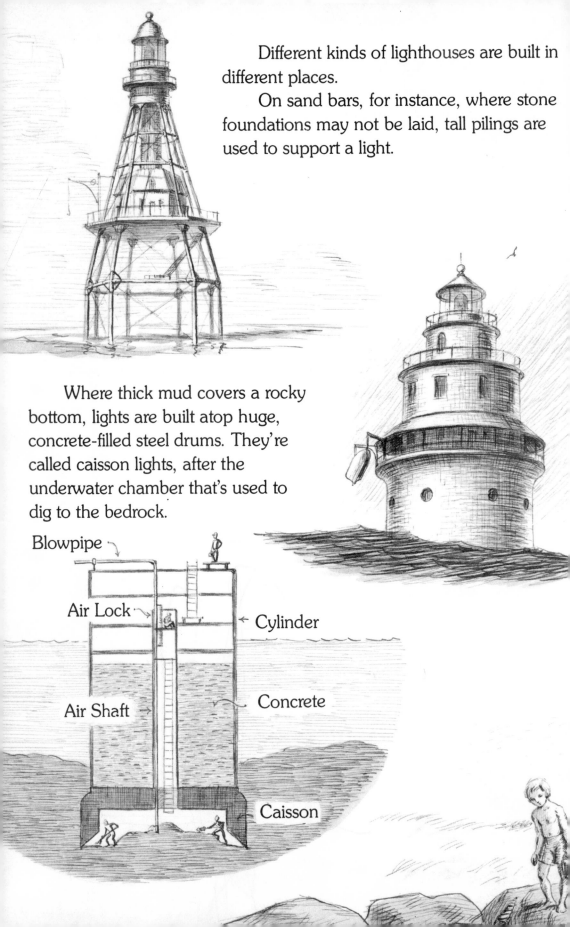

Different kinds of lighthouses are built in different places.

On sand bars, for instance, where stone foundations may not be laid, tall pilings are used to support a light.

Where thick mud covers a rocky bottom, lights are built atop huge, concrete-filled steel drums. They're called caisson lights, after the underwater chamber that's used to dig to the bedrock.

Blowpipe

Air Lock

Cylinder

Air Shaft

Concrete

Caisson

On cliffs and other spots where great height wasn't needed, lighthouses often were built in the form of ordinary houses. Years ago, keepers' families lived in them, but today most operate automatically, and their windows and doors have been boarded up.

Some lighthouses have flying buttresses like those of Medieval cathedrals. One of the largest, Father Point in Quebec, is in the middle of a small town—an odd contrast to the loneliness of most lighthouses.

Hotel St Lawrence

VACANCIES

Lightships have long been used
where lighthouses could not be built.
The earliest were ordinary ships
fitted with large lanterns. Because
they were often blown off their
stations, they were very dangerous.

Later, ships were designed just for this job.
But they were still dangerous. For instance, in
1936 in a dense fog, the lightship *Nantucket* was
struck and sunk by the liner *Olympic*.

Today, lightships are being replaced by new kinds of lighthouses. These modern descendants of the Pharos and the Eddystone may lack the grandeur and elegance of their ancestors, but they perform their functions well. And they continue the great tradition of lighting the dangers of the sea.